W9-DEU-337

Crafts That Celebrate

Celebrate

BLACK

HISTORY

By Kathy Ross
Illustrated by Jenny Stow

The Millbrook Press Brookfield, Connecticut

To Frances Ball

Library of Congress Cataloging-in-Publication Data
Ross, Kathy (Katharine Reynolds), 1948-
Crafts that celebrate black history / by Kathy Ross ; illustrated by Jenny Stow.
p. cm.
Summary: Provides step-by-step instructions for nineteen easy crafts which celebrate the accomplishments of different African Americans, including inventors, activists, educators, and others.
ISBN 0-7613-2515-8 (lib. bdg.) — ISBN 0-7613-1681-7 (pbk.)
1. Handicraft—Juvenile literature. 2. African Americans—Juvenile literature. [1. Handicraft. 2. African Americans.] I. Stow, Jenny, ill. II. Title.
TT160 .R71414 2002   745.594'1—dc21   2001044769

Published by The Millbrook Press, Inc.
2 Old New Milford Road
Brookfield, Connecticut 06804
www.millbrookpress.com

Printed in the United States of America
library 5 4 3 2 1
pbk   5 4 3 2 1

Photographs courtesy of
The Schomburg Center for Research in
Black Culture, The New York Public
Library: pp. 4, 7, 10, 14, 16, 39; Culver
Pictures, Inc.: pp. 12, 22, 36;
University of Chicago
Library/Department of Special
Collections: p. 18; Iowa State
University Library/Special Collections
Department: p. 20; Library of Congress:
p. 25 (USZ62-84495); National
Archives: pp. 27, 30, 42;
© Bettmann/Corbis: p. 32; A. Phillip
Randolph Institute: p. 34; AP/Wide
World Photos: p. 44, 46

Contents

BENJAMIN BANNEKER
(1731–1806)

Benjamin Banneker was a genius in the fields of mathematics, astronomy, and invention. His numerous accomplishments included making the first working clock in America, publishing a scientific almanac, and helping survey the land that was to become Washington, D.C.

Accomplishments of Benjamin Banneker

Here is what you need:

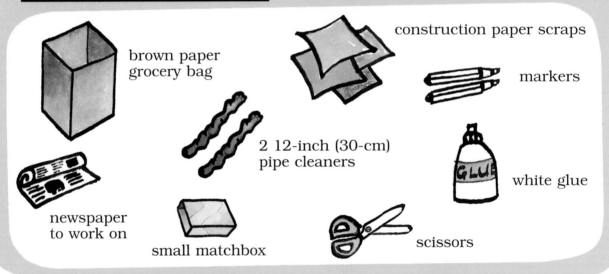

brown paper grocery bag

construction paper scraps

markers

2 12-inch (30-cm) pipe cleaners

white glue

newspaper to work on

small matchbox

scissors

Here is what you do:

1   Cut down the seam of the brown grocery bag. Cut out the bottom of the bag and discard it. You should be left with a long piece of brown paper. Fold the strip of brown paper in half so that the strip is half as long.

2 Draw the outline of Benjamin Banneker on one side of the folded paper with the arms sticking on each side. Cut out the outline out through both sides of the folded bag so that the figure has a front and a back piece.

3

Use the markers to add facial features and clothes to the front of the figure. You will also need to color the back of each arm because they will show when folded around to the front of the figure.

4

Cover the inside of the back piece of the figure with glue. Lay the pipe cleaners across the arms of the figure. Carefully fold and press the figure that you colored over the back piece to glue the two pieces together with the pipe cleaners between them.

5 Bend the two arms around to the front of the figure. Trim the edges of the figure to make the front and back paper even.

6 Cover the matchbox with construction paper. Make a paper clock face to glue on the front to make a clock. Cut a square of paper and write "Plans for Washington, D.C." on it. Fold a piece of paper in half like a book. Write "Almanac by Benjamin Banneker" on the cover. Glue the items behind the arms of the figure to look like they are being held by the figure.

Find out what else Benjamin Banneker achieved during his lifetime and add them to the armload of accomplishments.

SOJOURNER TRUTH
(1797–1883)

Sojourner Truth courageously traveled the country speaking out against slavery. Her intelligence and dramatic presentation style quickly gained her fame as a compelling and convincing speaker for the rights of black Americans.

Sojourner Truth Puppet

Here is what you need:

 3-inch (8-cm) Styrofoam ball

 newspaper to work on

 small brown pom-pom

 2 large wiggle eyes

 brown paint and a paintbrush

 black yarn

 craft stick

 piece of red felt, about 3 inches (8 cm) square

 white sock

 large paper clip

 white glue

 straight pins

 fabric

 scissors

 Styrofoam tray for drying

Here is what you do:

1 Ask an adult to cut off about 1/3 of the Styrofoam ball. The smaller piece will form the bottom jaw of the puppet and the top piece the upper jaw and the head.

2 Paint the outside of both pieces of the Styrofoam ball brown. Let the pieces dry on the Styrofoam tray.

3 Fold the red felt in half. Cut a half circle on the fold using the bottom jaw as a pattern.

4 Glue one half of the folded circle to one side of the bottom jaw and the other half of the circle to the cut edge of the second piece of the ball to join the top and bottom of the head together. The red felt will be the inside of the mouth.

5 Cut black yarn bits for hair. Glue the yarn bits to the top of the head.

Cut a 3-inch (8-cm) piece from the toe of the sock to use as a cap for the puppet. If it does not stay on by itself use some pins to secure it.

7 Glue on the two wiggle eyes and the pom-pom for a nose.

8 Cut a 9-by-18-inch (23-by-46-cm) rectangle of fabric for the dress for the puppet. Fold the fabric into a square. Put the craft stick between the front and back of the fabric at the center of the fold and push the stick up into the bottom of the puppet head to attach the dress to the head and make a holder for the puppet.

9 Push one end of the paper clip into the back of the top section of the head of the puppet to use as a handle for opening and closing the mouth.

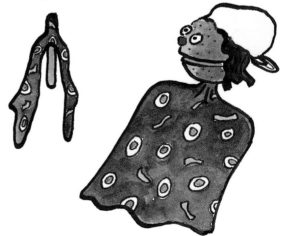

What do you think your Sojourner Truth puppet might say about slavery?

9

FREDERICK A. DOUGLASS
(1817–1895)

Frederick A. Douglass was an abolitionist. That means he was a man who was against slavery. His firsthand knowledge of what it was like to be a slave and his tremendous skill as a public speaker made him the most influential spokesman for black Americans of his time.

Talking Frederick A. Douglass Puppet

Here is what you need:

brown, red, and white construction paper

markers

fiberfill or cotton ball

white glue

cereal box cardboard

scissors

clamp clothespin

Here is what you do:

1

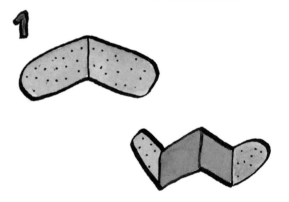

Cut an 8-by-3-inch (20-by-8-cm) strip of cardboard from the cereal box, rounding off the ends. Fold the cardboard in half with the print on the outside. About 2 inches (5 cm) from the fold, bend each side of the folded strip outward. The inside of the fold will be the inside of the mouth of the puppet. Cover the inside of the mouth with red construction paper.

Cut a 4-inch (10-cm) circle from the brown paper. Cut about 1/3 of the circle off one end. The small piece of the circle will form the bottom jaw of the puppet and the larger piece of the circle will form the top of the mouth and the head.

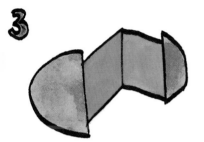

Glue the top and bottom of the head over the cardboard on each side of the mouth. There will be some excess cardboard sticking out on each end.

Cut two triangles from the white paper to make a shirt collar for the puppet. Glue the collar to the bottom edge of the head. Trim off any excess cardboard from the top and bottom of the head.

Use the markers to give the puppet eyes and a nose. Glue on white cotton or fiberfill for hair. Glue a clamp clothespin over the top and bottom of the mouth fold at the back of the puppet.

By pinching the clothespin you can open and shut the mouth of your Frederick Douglass puppet as it tells people why slavery is wrong.

11

HARRIET TUBMAN
(1820–1913)

Harriet Tubman was known as "the Moses of her people." Her courage and amazing knowledge of geography led her to establish the Underground Railroad, a series of safe homes along the route from the South to freedom in the North. She led more than 300 people to freedom, repeatedly risking her own life for others.

Route to Freedom Maze

Here is what you need:

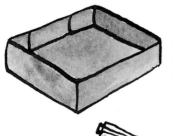 carton lid or shallow carton such as canned goods come in

 package of bendable straws

markers

 scissors

 white glue

 wooden bead about the size of a marble

 ballpoint pen

Here is what you do:

Turn the box so that it is longest from bottom to top. Use a marker to mark the four inside walls of the box N (north), S (south), E (east), and W (west) with north being at the top.

2 Use the straws to create a maze in the bottom of the carton. Cut the straws when necessary to get the lengths needed. Make sure the path of the maze is wide enough for the bead to pass through. Remember to make some paths that lead nowhere. Make only one path that leads from south (the bottom of the box) to north (the top of the box). Experiment with making your maze, moving the pieces of straw around to create different paths.

3 When you are satisfied with your maze, glue the pieces of straw in place.

4 Use the markers to draw "safe" houses along the path to the north.

5 Draw a star on the wooden bead. Harriet Tubman used the stars to find her way.

6 Use the ballpoint pen to poke a hole in the carton at the beginning of the maze and at the end.

Set the wooden bead in the hole in the carton at the start of the maze. Tilt the carton to roll the star through the maze to the north and freedom.

13

PAUL LAURENCE DUNBAR
(1872–1906)

Paul Laurence Dunbar has been called "the poet of his people." By writing poetry in black dialect he showed the great beauty to be found in this form of speech.

Paper and Pencil Magnet

Here is what you need:

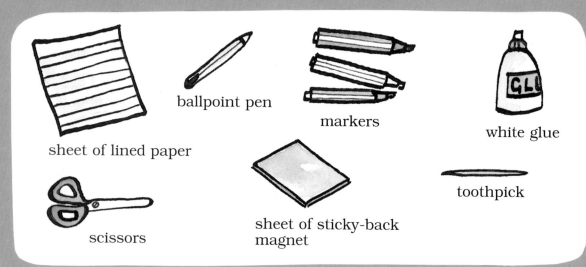

sheet of lined paper

ballpoint pen

markers

white glue

scissors

sheet of sticky-back magnet

toothpick

Here is what you do:

1

Cut a 2-by-3-inch (5-by-8-cm) piece of paper from the lined paper.

 Use the pen to add additional lines to the paper, leaving a space at the top like a full sized sheet of paper would have.

Write "Paul Laurence Dunbar" across the top of the paper. Write "Poet of his People" on the next line.

Write your own poem and use the magnet to hang it on the refrigerator.

Stick the tiny piece of paper to a sheet of sticky-back magnet. Trim around the paper so that the magnet is the exact same size.

Cut one end off the toothpick to make it about 1¾ inches (4.5 cm) long.

7 Glue the pencil to the paper.

Use the markers to color the toothpick to look like a pen or pencil.

GRANVILLE T. WOODS
(1856-1910)

Granville T. Woods was an inventor who held more than forty-five patents. One of his most important inventions was for a system of communication to be installed in trains so that they could communicate their locations in order to avoid colliding.

Granville T. Woods Invention Puzzle

Here is what you need:

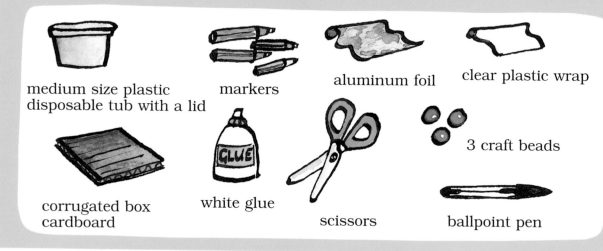

medium size plastic disposable tub with a lid

markers

aluminum foil

clear plastic wrap

corrugated box cardboard

white glue

scissors

3 craft beads

ballpoint pen

Here is what you do:

1

Use the bottom of the plastic tub to trace two circles on the corrugated box cardboard. Cut out the two circles. Trim the edges slightly, if necessary, to make them fit snugly inside the bottom of the tub.

2 Use the markers to draw three trains on a railroad track on one of the circles.

3 Use the ballpoint pen to poke a hole through the front of each train for a bead to rest in.

4 Glue the plain cardboard circle in the bottom of the tub. Glue the colored circle on top of the plain circle.

5 Cover the outside of the tub with aluminum foil. Fold the edges down over the top of the tub and trim them. Drop the three beads into the container.

6 Cut the inside circle out of the rim of the lid.

7 Cover the container with a piece of plastic wrap. Secure the wrap by snapping the rim of the lid on over it. Trim the edges of the plastic wrap to the outer edge of the rim.

Quick! Stop the trains from colliding by installing Granville T. Woods's invention (represented by the beads) in each train engine.

IDA B. WELLS-BARNETT
(1862–1931)

Ida B. Wells-Barnett was a journalist who showed astounding courage and commitment to attaining equal rights for all people, regardless of color or sex.

Ida B. Wells-Barnett's "All Kinds of People" Pin

Here is what you need:

yarn and thread bits in three different colors

white glue

6 tiny wiggle eyes, in three different colors if possible

3 natural-color craft beads

pin back

3 tiny pom-poms in three different colors

scissors

poster paint in three different skin tones and a paintbrush

Styrofoam tray to work on

Here is what you do:

1

Paint each bead a different color to make three different heads. Let the beads dry on the Styrofoam tray.

2

Give each bead hair in a different color by gluing some yarn or thread bits to the top of each bead.

3

Glue a pair of eyes and a pom-pom nose to the front of each bead to make a face for each one.

4

Glue the three different heads together.

Wear the pin and remember the words of Ida B. Wells-Barnett, who hoped that someday "human beings . . . pay tribute to what they believe one possesses in the way of qualities of mind and heart . . . rather than to the color of the skin." She wanted all people to be valued for what they did, no matter what they looked like.

5

Glue a pin back to the back of the heads.

GEORGE WASHINGTON CARVER
(c. 1860–1943)

George Washington Carver was a scientist of phenomenal creativity and genius. Perhaps the most famous among his enormous number of contributions to the scientific world of agriculture is his discovery of hundreds of new uses for the peanut.

"Thank you, George Washington Carver" Magn

Here is what you need:

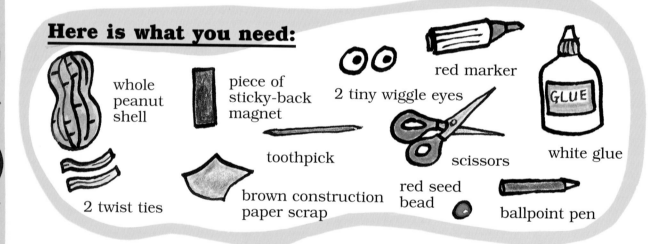

whole peanut shell

piece of sticky-back magnet

2 tiny wiggle eyes

red marker

GLUE

white glue

toothpick

scissors

2 twist ties

brown construction paper scrap

red seed bead

ballpoint pen

Here is what you do:

1 Glue the center of one twist tie to the middle of the back of the peanut so that the two ends stick out to form arms. If the arms seem too long, trim them.

2 Bend the second twist tie in half to form an upside-down V-shape for the legs. Bend the two ends up for feet. Glue the fold of the twist tie to the back of the peanut below the arms so that the legs hang down from the back of the peanut.

3 Cut a small square from the brown paper for a flag. Write "Thank you, George Washington Carver" on the flag. Glue the flag to one end of the toothpick. Wrap the end of one arm around the end of the toothpick to make it look like the peanut is holding the flag. Secure the toothpick to the arm with glue.

4 Cut two tiny hands for the peanut arms from the brown paper. Glue a hand to the end of each arm.

5 Glue the two wiggle eyes to the top part of the peanut. Glue the red seed bead below the eyes for a nose. Use the red marker to draw a smile on the peanut.

6 Press a piece of sticky-back magnet to the back of the peanut.

Hang the peanut on the refrigerator to remember George Washington Carver. Among the many products he made from peanuts were paper, shaving cream, plastics, and ink. Find out what else he made from the peanut.

MATTHEW A. HENSON
(1866–1955)

Matthew A. Henson was an explorer
and the first man to actually arrive
and stand on the North Pole.

Matthew A. Henson on the North Pole

Here is what you need:

paper bowl

brown pipe
cleaners

white glue

brown, yellow,
and white
construction
paper scraps

fiberfill

markers

scissors

Here is what you do:

1 Turn the
bowl over
and cover the
bottom by
gluing on fiberfill to look like a mound of snow.

2 Cut a 2-by-3-inch (5-by-8-cm) piece of white paper. Use the markers to color the paper to look like the American flag.

Glue the flag to one end of a 6-inch (15-cm) piece of pipe cleaner. Bend the bottom end of the pipe cleaner and glue it under the fiberfill at the center of the bowl to look like it is planted in the snow.

3  Bend a 4-inch (10-cm) piece of pipe cleaner in half to make legs for the figure of Matthew Henson. Bend the ends to make feet. Cut a 2-inch (5-cm) piece of pipe cleaner. Wrap the center of the pipe cleaner around the fold of the legs so that the ends stick out on each side for arms.

4  Fold the yellow construction paper in half. Trace around the pipe cleaner arms and legs to make a snowsuit for the figure. Cut out the suit on the folded paper so that you get a front and back for the suit. Glue the suit to the front and the back of the pipe-cleaner figure.

5  Cut a head for the figure from the brown paper. Use the markers to draw a face on one side. Glue fiberfill around the face to look like a fur hood to the snowsuit. Glue the head to the top of the snowsuit.

6 Stand the figure in the "snow" next to the flag and wrap the end of one pipe-cleaner arm around the flagpole to support the figure in a standing position.

7 Make a paper label for the front of the display that says "Matthew A. Henson, Explorer, First Man to Stand on the North Pole."

Matthew A. Henson, Explorer, First Man to Stand on the North Pole.

Some people may be surprised to hear that Matthew A. Henson, not Robert Peary, was actually the first man to reach the North Pole.

W. E. B. Du Bois
(1868–1963)

W. E. B. Du Bois, a sociologist of tremendous intellect, fought for recognition of the abilities and contributions of black Americans and the equal rights they were entitled to. He is perhaps best known for his role in founding the National Association for the Advancement of Colored People (NAACP).

File Box of Black American Heroes

Here is what you need:

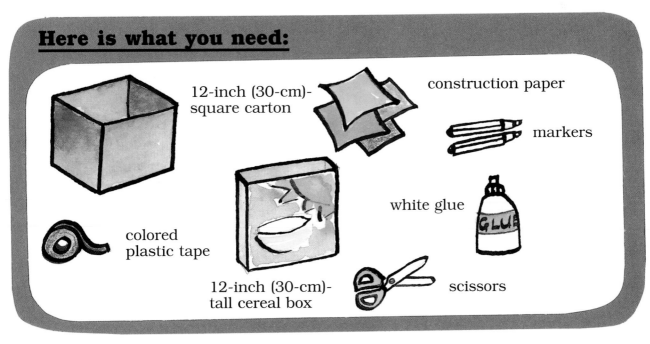

12-inch (30-cm)-square carton

construction paper

markers

colored plastic tape

white glue

12-inch (30-cm)-tall cereal box

scissors

Here is what you do:

Cut a piece of construction paper to fit over each side of the carton to cover it. Use the markers to decorate the construction paper with people from black American history.

2 Glue the papers to the sides of the box to cover it. Wrap the top edge of the box with the plastic tape to give the file box a more finished look.Cut out one side of the cereal box. Glue the top of the box closed. Glue the cereal box in the center of the file box, uncut side down, to create a divider inside the box. You can create more sections in the box if you wish by adding more cereal box dividers.

3

Make file folders for the file box by folding large sheets of construction paper in half.

Collect information about black Americans from the Web and from newspaper and magazine articles. Write the name of each person you find information about on a separate file folder. As you find new information about a person, store the papers in the correct file. Place the files in your file box in alphabetical order to allow you to locate a person quickly and easily.

JAMES WELDON JOHNSON
(1871–1938)

James Weldon Johnson, a multitalented writer, went through the South gathering and recording the music and literature of the black culture. His efforts contributed enormously to the understanding of the struggle of the black people, and the preservation of their heritage.

James Weldon Johnson Collection Game

Here is what you need:

small food box such as individual cereal servings come in

cereal box cardboard

pipe cleaners

yarn

scissors

glue

white and blue construction paper

marker

hole punch

Here is what you do:

1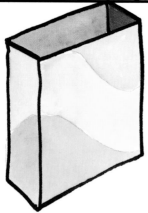

Cut the top off the food box. Punch a hole in the center of the top edge of the front and back of the box.

2

Cut a 2-inch (5-cm) circle from the cereal box cardboard. Use the marker to write the word "stories" on the circle. Punch a hole in the top of the circle.

3

Shape a musical note from a piece of the pipe cleaner. Make it 2 inches (5 cm) high.

4

Cut two 1-foot (30-cm) lengths of yarn. To make the game harder, cut longer pieces of yarn. To make the game easier cut shorter pieces of yarn.

5

Tie one end of a piece of yarn through one of the holes in the top edge of the box. Tie the cardboard circle of "stories" to the other end. Tie the other piece of yarn through the other hole in the edge of the box. Tie on the music note.

Make the box look like a book by cutting a piece of blue construction paper large enough to cover three sides of the box and extend over the edge about ¼-inch (.5 cm). Glue the paper to the box. Cut a strip of white construction paper to cover the fourth side of the box to make it look like the pages of a closed book. On the front of the book write "James Weldon Johnson collected and recorded the songs and stories of black Americans."

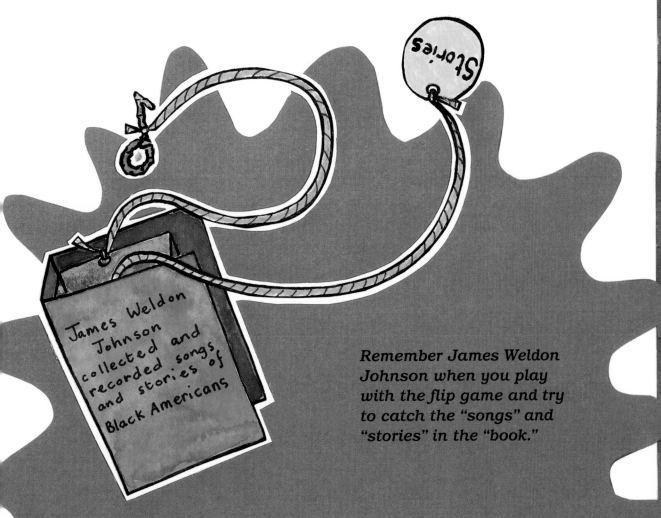

James Weldon Johnson collected and recorded songs and stories of Black Americans

Remember James Weldon Johnson when you play with the flip game and try to catch the "songs" and "stories" in the "book."

MARY MCLEOD BETHUNE
(1875–1955)

Mary McLeod Bethune was an educator who, with only $1.50, founded a school for black Americans that grew to become Bethune-Cookman College in Daytona Beach, Florida.

Mary McLeod Bethune's School that Grew

Here is what you need:

 small box such as jewelry comes in

 roll of adding-machine tape

 scissors

 markers

white glue

Here is what you do:

1

Stand the box on one of the short ends to become a building. Cut a piece of adding-machine tape slightly longer than the height of the lid of the box. Cut one end of the tape into a triangle roof. Use the markers to draw a school building on the paper. Glue the building to the lid of the box.

Cut a strip of paper 8 to 12 inches (20 to 30 cm) long. Fold the paper like a fan, with each section the width of the box building. Draw more buildings across the paper. Write "Bethune-Cookman College" across the top of the paper.

Glue one end of the paper inside the lid of the box. Glue the other end inside the bottom of the box.

Make a sign that says "With only $1.50 Mary McLeod Bethune started a school for blacks that grew to become a college." Glue the sign to the bottom of the box.

Stand the box on end and pull the bottom of the box to one side to show how the tiny school became a big college because Mary McLeod Bethune had the courage to pursue her dream.

31

CARTER G. WOODSON
(1875–1950)

Carter G. Woodson has been called the "Father of Black History." He fought to get recognition of the enormous contributions to society made by black Americans. He was responsible for establishing Black History Week in 1926. Today we celebrate Black History Month in February.

Timeline of Black American Heroes

Here is what you need:

 construction paper

cereal box cardboard

 white glue

 drinking glass to use as circle pattern

 paper clips

ballpoint pen

 small hole punch

markers or small pictures printed off the Web

 markers

Here is what you do:

1 Trace around the rim of the drinking glass on the cardboard. Cut the circle out to use as a pattern. Use the pattern to cut several circles from construction paper.

32

2 Write the name of a famous black American on each circle. Write down the dates of their birth and death so you will know when they lived in history.

3 Use the markers to draw a small picture of each person or print a small picture off the Web to glue on the circle. Write a small description of what the person did under the picture.

4 Punch a small hole in each side of each circle. Join the circles together with paper clips to make a long line of circles. Put the people in order according to when they lived. You might want to make the first circle of the timeline say "February is Black History Month."

5 Hang the timeline using the paperclips at each end.

As you learn about more black American heroes you can easily add them to the correct place on the timeline.

33

A. PHILIP RANDOLPH
(1889–1979)

Among the numerous achievements of A. Philip Randolph was his success in organizing the Brotherhood of Sleeping Car Porters. This was the first successful attempt to bring a group of black workers together to gain a contract providing fairer wages and working conditions from a white employer.

Brotherhood of Sleeping Car Porters Puzzle

Here is what you need:

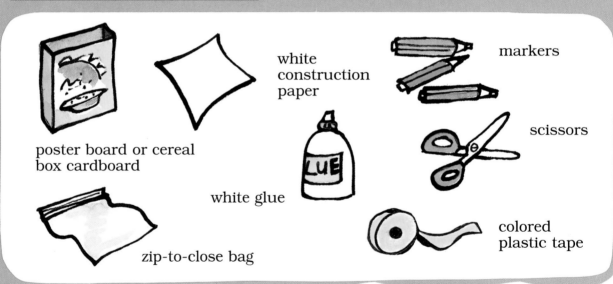

poster board or cereal box cardboard

white construction paper

markers

white glue

scissors

zip-to-close bag

colored plastic tape

Here is what you do:

1 Cut the construction paper to the size you would like the puzzle to be. Write "Brotherhood of Sleeping Car Porters" across the top of the paper. It was the job of the train porters to assist the passengers with luggage and other needs while traveling on the train. Draw several black American train porters with trains in the background.

2 Glue the paper to the poster board. Trim the edges of the poster board around the picture so the poster board does not show. Let the glue dry.

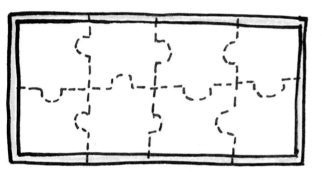

3 Cover the edges of the puzzle with the colored plastic tape to give it a finished look.

4 Draw the pieces of the puzzle on the back of the picture. Make about nine to twelve pieces. Cut out the puzzle pieces. Store the pieces in the zip-to-close bag.

When you put the pieces of the puzzle together to join the many sleeping car porters, remember A. Philip Randolph.

LOUIS "SATCHMO" ARMSTRONG
(c. 1900–1971)

Best known as Louie, Armstrong was a world-famous jazz trumpeter.

Louie Armstrong Puppet

Here is what you need:

 newspaper to work on

9-inch (23-cm) uncoated paper plate

 BROWN POSTER — brown poster paint and a paintbrush

 yellow and red construction paper

 black marker

 black yarn

 GLUE — white glue

cereal box cardboard

 masking tape

party horn

 scissors

Here is what you do:

1 Paint the bottom side of the paper plate brown. Let it dry. This will become the face for the puppet.

2 Cut some black yarn bits for hair. Glue the hair to the top edge of the painted plate.

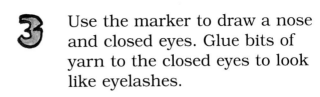

3 Use the marker to draw a nose and closed eyes. Glue bits of yarn to the closed eyes to look like eyelashes.

4 Cut a 2-inch (5-cm) circle from the red paper for a mouth. Glue the mouth to the plate face.

5 Fold the yellow paper in half. Drawa trumpet on the paper. Cut out the trumpet through both sides of the paper so it has two sides. Use the marker to add details to both sides of the trumpet.

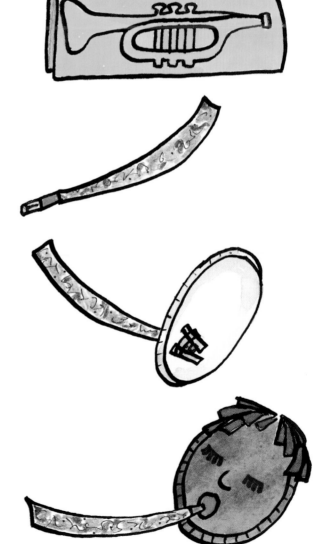

6 Flatten out the cardboard part of the party horn. Poke a small hole through the mouth of the puppet. Insert the mouthpiece of the horn through the front of the mouth so it sticks out in back of the puppet. Use masking tape to hold the horn in place.

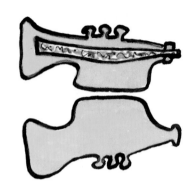

Glue the two sides of the paper trumpet together over the crushed horn, with the mouth end of the trumpet glued around the horn piece sticking out from the mouth so that it looks like the puppet is blowing the trumpet.

8

Use the marker to draw puffed-out cheeks on each side of the puppet's mouth to make it look like the puppet is blowing on the trumpet. Write "Louie Armstrong" on the back of the puppet.

Make a horn sound by blowing on the mouthpiece of the party horn at the back of the puppet.

MARIAN ANDERSON
(1902–1993)

Marian Anderson was a famous opera singer who was called "The Century's Contralto" because of her beautiful and powerful singing voice.

Singing Marian Anderson Puppet

Here is what you need:

two cardboard toilet tissue tubes

craft stick

fabric

black yarn

rubber band

ribbon

markers

scissors

masking tape

white glue

Here is what you do:

Cut up one side of one of the cardboard tubes. Glue the end of the craft stick inside the bottom of the tube to form a handle sticking out from the bottom of the tube. Secure it with masking tape.

Insert the cut tube inside the second tube so that the top 2 inches (5 cm) of the tube stick out from the top of the second tube to form the head of the puppet and the stick handle protrudes from the bottom of the tube.

Use the markers to draw eyes and a nose on the head. Draw a small round mouth with the top of the mouth on the inner tube and the bottom of the mouth on the outer tube.

Use the stick to push the inner tube up about 1/4 inch (1/2 cm). Fill in the area between the top and bottom parts of the mouth to look like an open mouth. The mouth should now open and close by pushing and pulling on the stick.

Close the opening at the top of the head using masking tape. Glue black yarn over the tape, back, and sides of the head for hair.

6 Cut a rectangle of fabric large enough to wrap around the puppet below the mouth and hide the bottom part of the tube and the handle. Wrap the fabric around the neck of the puppet and hold it in place with a rubber band. Tie a piece of ribbon in a bow over the rubber band to hide it.

Push the stick of the puppet up and down to make the Marian Anderson puppet sing.

RALPH JOHNSON BUNCHE
(1904–1971)

Ralph Johnson Bunche, the first black American to receive the Nobel Peace Prize, was an internationally known diplomat.

Ralph Johnson Bunche Bookmark

Here is what you need:

old jigsaw puzzle pieces

Styrofoam tray to work on

thin ribbon

sharp black marker

construction paper

craft bead

white poster paint and a paintbrush

white glue

scissors

crinkle-cut scissors

Here is what you do:

1 Use the scissors to trim two puzzle pieces to resemble the shape of a flying bird. Paint both sides of the two puzzle pieces white to look like doves. The dove is a symbol of peace. Let them dry on the Styrofoam tray.

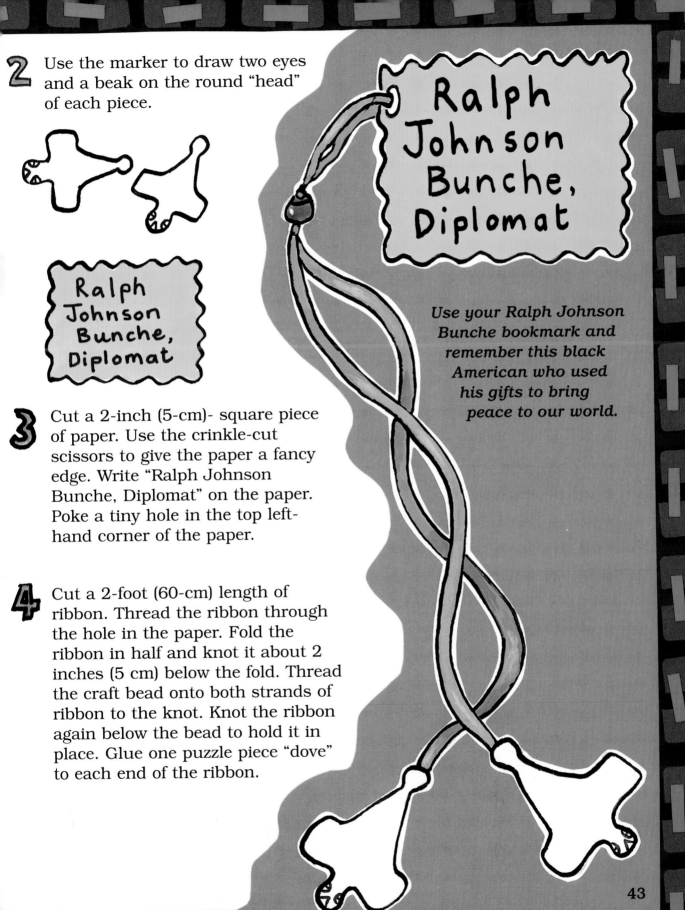

2 Use the marker to draw two eyes and a beak on the round "head" of each piece.

Ralph Johnson Bunche, Diplomat

3 Cut a 2-inch (5-cm)- square piece of paper. Use the crinkle-cut scissors to give the paper a fancy edge. Write "Ralph Johnson Bunche, Diplomat" on the paper. Poke a tiny hole in the top left-hand corner of the paper.

4 Cut a 2-foot (60-cm) length of ribbon. Thread the ribbon through the hole in the paper. Fold the ribbon in half and knot it about 2 inches (5 cm) below the fold. Thread the craft bead onto both strands of ribbon to the knot. Knot the ribbon again below the bead to hold it in place. Glue one puzzle piece "dove" to each end of the ribbon.

Ralph Johnson Bunche, Diplomat

Use your Ralph Johnson Bunche bookmark and remember this black American who used his gifts to bring peace to our world.

JESSE OWENS
(1913–1980)

Jesse Owens discredited racial prejudices and attracted worldwide attention at the 1936 Summer Olympic Games by breaking three world records and winning four gold medals.

Running Jesse Owens

Here is what you need:

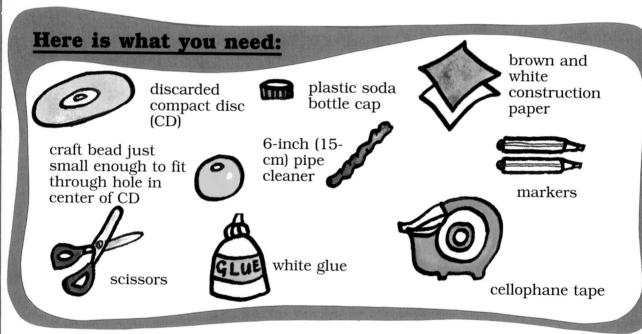

discarded compact disc (CD)

plastic soda bottle cap

brown and white construction paper

craft bead just small enough to fit through hole in center of CD

6-inch (15-cm) pipe cleaner

markers

scissors

white glue

cellophane tape

Here is what you do:

1 Glue the craft bead to the center of the top of the plastic cap. Let the glue dry.

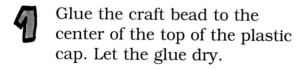

2 Set the CD over the bead on the plastic cap. It should spin around freely on the bead.

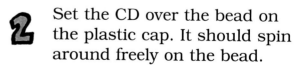

3

Cut a 2-by-3-inch (5-by-8-cm) piece of white paper for a flag. Draw the Olympic symbol on the flag with the markers. Glue the flag to one end of the pipe cleaner. Glue the other end of the pipe cleaner into the bead to mount the Olympic flag in the center of the CD.

4

On the brown construction paper, draw a figure, 2 to 3 inches (5 to 8 cm) tall, of Jesse Owens running. Add details and color the figure with the markers. Draw a 1/2-inch (1.25-cm) paper tab on the bottom of the figure to be used to attach the figure to the CD. Cut out the figure with the tab at the bottom.

5

Bend the tab toward the back of the figure. Tape the tab to the edge of the CD.

Hold the cap and spin the CD to see Jesse Owens run a few victory laps around the Olympic flag.

MARTIN LUTHER KING, JR.
(1929–1968)

Martin Luther King, Jr., a minister and the most influential civil rights leader of modern history, wanted a country where people of all colors lived together as brothers and sisters.

All One Family Necklace

Here is what you need:

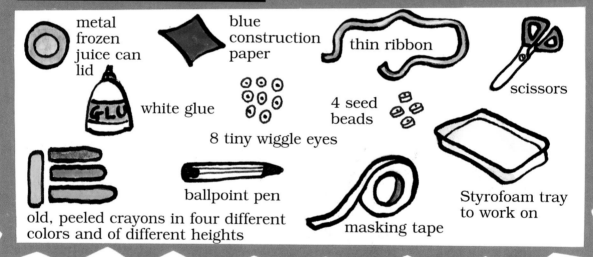

metal frozen juice can lid

blue construction paper

thin ribbon

scissors

white glue

4 seed beads

8 tiny wiggle eyes

old, peeled crayons in four different colors and of different heights

ballpoint pen

masking tape

Styrofoam tray to work on

Here is what you do:

1

Trace around the metal lid on the blue paper. Cut the paper circle out. Cover one side of the lid with some strips of masking tape to create a stronger gluing surface. Glue the paper to the tape-covered side of the lid. Use the pen to write "All One Family" across the top of the paper circle.

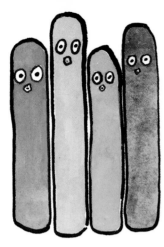

2 Glue the four crayons, side-by-side, to the paper-covered lid to represent four different people.

3 Give each crayon a face by gluing on two tiny wiggle eyes and a seed bead nose.

4 Cut a 2-foot (60-cm) length of ribbon. Glue the two ends of the ribbon to the back of the lid to make a necklace. Secure the ribbon with masking tape.

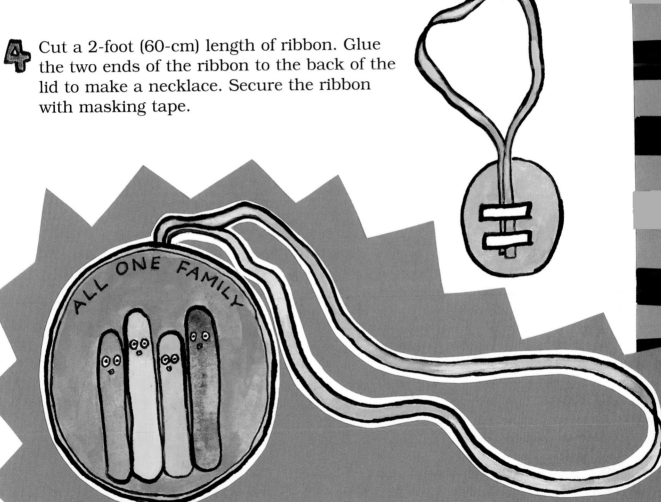

ALL ONE FAMILY

Wear your necklace on January 15, the birthday of Martin Luther King, Jr. and a national holiday.

ABOUT THE AUTHOR AND ARTIST

Twenty-five years as a teacher and director of nursery school programs have given Kathy Ross extensive experience in guiding young children through craft projects. Among the more than thirty-five craft books she has written are CRAFTS FOR ALL SEASONS, MAKE YOURSELF A MONSTER, CRAFTS FROM YOUR FAVORITE FAIRY TALES, and CRAFTS FROM YOUR FAVORITE CHILDREN'S SONGS. Her popular series include *Holiday Crafts for Kids, Crafts for Kids Who are Wild About...,* and *Play-Doh® Fun.*

When Kathy is not having fun making craft projects or working writing books, she travels across the country doing craft programs for schools and libraries. If you would like to see more of her crafts, visit her at www.kathyross.com.

Jenny Stow is a graduate of the University of London and has her Masters in Education from the University of Bristol in England. A special education teacher by vocation, she is the illustrator of a number of picture books, among them THE HOUSE THAT JACK BUILT and THE COMING OF NIGHT.